Pebble

Families

Revised
and
Updated

Cousins

by Lola M. Schaefer

Consulting Editor: Gail Saunders-Smith, PhD

Capstone
press®
Mankato, Minnesota

Pebble Books are published by Capstone Press,
151 Good Counsel Drive, P.O. Box 669, Mankato, Minnesota 56002.
www.capstonepress.com

1 2 3 4 5 6 13 12 11 10 09 08

Library of Congress Cataloging-in-Publication Data
Schaefer, Lola M., 1950–
  Cousins/by Lola M. Schaefer. — Rev. and updated ed.
  p. cm. — (Pebble books. Families)
  Summary: "Simple text and photographs present cousins and how they interact
with their families" — Provided by publisher.
  Includes bibliographical references and index.
  ISBN-13: 978-1-4296-1222-7 (hardcover)
  ISBN-10: 1-4296-1222-3 (hardcover)
  ISBN-13: 978-1-4296-1751-2 (softcover)
  ISBN-10: 1-4296-1751-9 (softcover)
  1. Cousins — Juvenile literature. I. Title. II. Series.
HQ759.97.S33 2008
306.87 — dc22   2007027027

Note to Parents and Teachers

The Families set supports national social studies standards related
to identifying family members and their roles. This book describes
and illustrates cousins. The images support early readers in
understanding the text. The repetition of words and phrases helps
early readers learn new words. This book also introduces early
readers to subject-specific vocabulary words, which are defined
in the glossary section. Early readers may need some assistance to
read some words and to use the Table of Contents, Glossary, Read
More, Internet Sites, and Index sections of the book.

Table of Contents

Cousins

Cousins are children
of aunts and uncles.

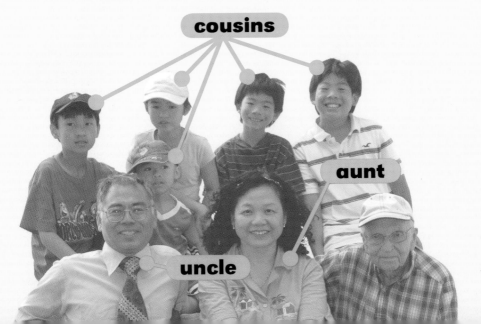

cousins

aunt

uncle

Some cousins are girls.

Some cousins are boys.

Cousins Visit

Andy's cousins visit
on his birthday.

Abby's cousins visit during summer vacation.

Being Together

Alice and her cousin play at a park.

Will and his cousin
eat pizza.

Ivy and her cousins have sleepovers.

Vera and her cousins carve pumpkins.

Cousins have fun.

Glossary

aunt — your mother's or father's sister

carve — to cut a shape or slices out of something; people carve faces into pumpkins.

uncle — your mother's or father's brother

vacation — a time of rest away from school, work, or other daily activities; vacations are sometimes trips away from home.

Read More

Easterling, Lisa. *Families.* Our Global Community. Chicago: Heinemann, 2007.

West, Colin. *Uncle Pat and Auntie Pat.* Read-it! Chapter Books. Minneapolis: Picture Window Books, 2006.

Internet Sites

FactHound offers a safe, fun way to find Internet sites related to this book. All of the sites on FactHound have been researched by our staff.

Here's how:

1. Visit *www.facthound.com*
2. Choose your grade level.
3. Type in this book ID **1429612223** for age-appropriate sites. You may also browse subjects by clicking on letters, or by clicking on pictures and words.
4. Click on the **Fetch It** button.

FactHound will fetch the best sites for you!

Index

Word Count: 56
Grade 1
Early-Intervention Level: 10

Editorial Credits
Sarah L. Schuette, revised edition editor; Kim Brown, revised edition designer

Photo Credits
Capstone Press/Karon Dubke, all